LNER ALBUM
Volume One

Gresley masterpiece. Class A1 Pacific No 1478N, later named *Hermit*, stands in platform 10 at Kings Cross after arrival with an express from Leeds in 1924.

[*F. R. Hebron*

BRIAN STEPHENSON

LNER ALBUM

Volume One

LONDON

IAN ALLAN

First published 1970

SBN 7110 0155 3

Published by Ian Allan Ltd, Shepperton, Surrey,
and printed in the United Kingdom by Crampton & Sons Ltd, Sawston, Cambridge

Introduction

THE LONDON & NORTH EASTERN RAILWAY came to life on January 1, 1923 formed as a result of the Railways Act 1921 and was the second largest of the four groups created under the Act. The constituent companies which formed the LNER were, in order of route mileage: North Eastern Railway, North British Railway, Great Eastern Railway, Great Northern Railway, Great Central Railway, Great North of Scotland Railway, Hull & Barnsley Railway.

The last mentioned H & BR had amalgamated with the NER on April 1, 1922 under the provisions of the Act, and had thus lost its separate identity when the grouping took place.

Although the NER was by far the largest constituent the post of Chief Mechanical Engineer was given to Nigel Gresley, then CME of the GNR and it was the exploits of his locomotives for which the LNER is probably best remembered. At first pregrouping designs continued to be built in large numbers and amongst these were included Gresley's own GNR A1 Pacifics and K3 Moguls and so his big engine policy was to continue throughout the life of the LNER. So much so that there were seventy Gresley Pacifics operating on the East Coast main line before the first Pacific appeared on the rival West Coast route.

The first new designs to appear after the grouping were the class P1 freight Mikados and the class U1 2-8-8-2 Beyer Garratt locomotive for banking duties on the Worsborough incline. Both these appeared in time to take their place in the Railway Centenary procession on the old Stockton & Darlington line in 1925. Next the o-6-os of class J38 and J39 were to emerge from Darlington followed shortly by the D49 4-4-0s. Meanwhile as a result of the GWR-LNER locomotive trials of 1925 which showed that the A1 Pacifics were achieving results more by brute force than mechanical efficiency, many improvements were made to these engines which resulted in the new class A3 " Super Pacifics ". 1928

saw the class B17 " Sandringham " 4-6-0s take the road on the Great Eastern section whilst the following year Gresley's unsuccessful experimental water tube boiler 4-6-4 appeared.

In 1934 the first of Gresley's class P2 Mikados, No. 2001 Cock o' the North, was completed at Doncaster for service on the Aberdeen-Edinburgh line. They were to be the only eight-coupled express engines built for service in this country. The following year the first A4 Pacific was to make its amazing debut on the " Silver Jubilee ". This was Britain's first streamlined express which linked Newcastle with London in four hours at an average speed of 67.08 mph. It was after this crowning success that Gresley received the Knighthood " As engineer and speeder-up to the LNER " as is quoted from The Times by O. S. Nock in his book The Locomotives of Sir Nigel Gresley. Two further streamlined expresses were introduced in 1937, the " Coronation " with its beaver tail observation car and the " West Riding Limited ". 1936 saw the first examples of the class V2 Prairies built; this was to be Gresley's last big engine and was dubbed the engine that won the war—at least for the LNER it certainly was.

Sir Nigel Gresley died on April 5, 1941 and was succeeded by Edward Thompson who was steeped in the practices of the old NER, believing in rugged simple engines which were easy to maintain. His most notable design was the mixed traffic class B1 4-6-0 which was built in large numbers. Under his direction the P2 Mikados were rebuilt as somewhat ungainly Pacifics which together with the rebuilding of Gresley's first Pacific No. 4470 Great Northern, was considered as nothing less than vandalism by admirers of Gresley engines. Amongst other rebuilds carried out were the successful class O1 2-8-0s and the much needed class Q1 0-8-0 heavy shunting tanks.

Thompson retired in 1946 and Arthur H. Peppercorn took over for the short period before nationalisation on January 1, 1948.

Thompson designs continued in production but Peppercorn was, however, able to produce two fine Pacific designs in this time although the second did not appear until after the advent of British Railways.

The LNER had a difficult life mainly because it served the depressed area of the North East. The slump hit the company so badly that even the staff and unions agreed to accept a cut in wages for a period of two years. Unlike other railways in Britain it was unable to embark on the large scale replacement of older pregrouping locomotives employed on goods and secondary passenger services due to the financial restrictions. Fortunately most of these engines were of sound design and many lasted to the end of the steam era. Only seventeen new engines were built in 1933 whilst 34 had been built the previous year. Even during the worst years of the war new production did not drop quite so low.

Notwithstanding the depression the LNER did not rest on its laurels and in the field of record breaking it became a past master. On May 1, 1928 the non-stop "Flying Scotsman" was introduced over the 392 mile run from Kings Cross to Edinburgh. This was the world's longest regular non-stop journey and was made possible by the unique use of corridor tenders to allow engine crews to change over en-route without stopping. In March 1935 A3 Pacific No. 2750 *Papyrus* attained a maximum speed of 108 mph, finally breaking the long-standing GWR record set up by *City of Truro* in 1904, whilst on a high-speed trial run to see if it was possible to reach Kings Cross in four hours from Newcastle prior to the introduction of the "Silver Jubilee". With the introduction of the A4 Pacifics speeds crept up until on July 3, 1938 No. 4468 *Mallard* achieved the world speed record for steam traction of 126 mph, narrowly beating the 124.5 mph record set up by Deutsche Reichsbahn 4-6-4 No. 05 002 in 1936. With the out-

break of war in 1939 the LNER found itself in the front line serving the East Coast and suffered heavily at the hands of the Luftwaffe and later from the German flying bombs. It is said that one in seven of these V weapons fell either on LNER property or disrupted train services in some way.

Today all these things are but a memory and in this volume, the first of a two part album of LNER trains and locomotives, I have tried to compile a representative selection of pictures dating from the first years after the grouping to the last years of steam under British Railways in what was known as the Southern Area of the LNER which embraced the lines of the former Great Central, Great Eastern and Great Northern Railways. It is a pity they cannot be seen in colour, the apple green Pacifics hauling long trains of varnished teak coaches, the silver grey of the first A4s and the garter blue later adopted.

I am deeply indebted to F. R. Hebron, T. G. Hepburn, C. R. L. Coles, J. G. Dewing and E. E. Smith for supplying the major portion of the pictures, also to N. Fields for supplying prints taken by the late R. D. Pollard, to G. M. Kichenside for his help with the E. R. Wethersett plates and other prints taken from the publisher's files and to E. A. Wilkinson for helping with pictures from the LCGB Ken Nunn Collection. My thanks also go to the photographers who supplied the remaining photographs without which this book would not be complete. Final thanks go to my patient wife who has had to endure many late nights giving me moral support whilst I worked in the darkroom producing seemingly endless quantities of prints from the glass plates on which so many of these pictures were taken and for her ready assistance as critic, typist and proof reader.

March 1970

B.W.L.S.

Following the success of the first two Gresley three-cylinder Pacifics the GNR ordered a further ten from Doncaster which did not appear until after the grouping.   The first of these was No 1472 named *Flying Scotsman* in 1924 before being exhibited at the British Empire Exhibition at Wembley.   *Flying Scotsman*, now renumbered 4472 and with the LNER coat of arms on the cabsides but still retaining the handsome GNR chimney, leaves Wood Green Tunnel early in 1925 on its first run up to Kings Cross after the Wembley exhibition with an express from Grantham.   [*F. R. Hebron*

The final A1 of the 1923 batch No 1481N (the N suffix was used before the addition of 3000 to the numbers of GNR engines), later named *St Simon*, approaches Greenwood box with the 4 pm Kings Cross-Leeds express in 1924.   [*F. R. Hebron*

ABOVE: After trials against the Raven NER Pacifics the Gresley A1s were adopted as a standard class and a further forty were ordered in 1924. No 2549 *Persimmon* passes Ganwick box with a nineteen vehicle Sunday express from Leeds in 1927. [F. R. Hebron]

BELOW: No 2552, later named *Sansovino*, climbs past Finsbury Park with the 4.15 pm Kings Cross-Doncaster semi-fast in May 1925. Nos 2543-62 were built at Doncaster and Nos 2563-82 by the North British Locomotive Co Ltd. [F. R. Hebron]

UPPER LEFT: During the GWR-LNER locomotive exchange, which lasted from April 29 to May 4, 1925, GWR Castle class 4-6-0 No 4079 *Pendennis Castle* departs from Kings Cross with the 10.12 am Peterborough slow at the start of the exchange. No 4079s superior performance on LNER metals was to have a far-reaching effect on the expanding fleet of Gresley Pacifics. [*F. R. Hebron*

LOWER LEFT: Class A1 4-6-2 No 4474, later named *Victor Wild*, departs from Paddington with the 1.30 pm Exeter express. The first result of the exchange was the modification in 1926 of the short travel valve gear of Pacific No 4477 *Gay Crusader* so as to give longer laps. Next step early in 1927 was the complete redesign of the valve gear which was first tried on No 2555 *Centenary*. The new long travel valve gear much improved the performance of *Centenary* and the entire class was altered to this arrangement. The final step was to increase the boiler pressure from 180lb to 220lb thus creating a new class (see page 20). [*F. R. Hebron*

BELOW: Class A1 4-6-2 No 4472 *Flying Scotsman*, now cut down to the LNER composite load gauge, arrives at Kings Cross with the up "Flying Scotsman" in 1935. This was one of several A1s fitted with corridor tenders in 1928 for working the non-stop "Flying Scotsman". From this date engine numbers were moved from the tender to the cabsides to enable the easier exchange of tenders. [*C. R. L. Coles*

ABOVE: Class A1 4-6-2 No 2548 *Galtee More* stands in platform six at Kings Cross after arrival with an evening express in 1937. The engine is carrying the "Night Scotsman" headboard in readiness for its next duty. Note the poster advertising new houses and bungalows at Edgware from £755 freehold and £650 leasehold! [*E. E. Smith*

UPPER LEFT: Shortly before World War II several A1 Pacifics were transferred to the Great Central section for service between Manchester and Marylebone. No 4478 *Hermit* is seen at the head of the 3.20 pm Marylebone-Manchester express on the Met & GC joint line near Northwood in 1939. [*C. R. L. Coles*

LOWER LEFT: Class A1 4-6-2 No 2558 *Tracery*, fitted with a new high-sided non-corridor tender, departs from Nottingham Victoria with the 2.20 pm Manchester-Marylebone express in May 1939. [*T. G. Hepburn*

ABOVE: Another Gresley GNR design adopted as standard was his three-cylinder class K3 2-6-0. No 120 accelerates past Greenwood box after having waited on the slow line for an express to clear the notorious bottleneck in 1925. This was one of fifty K3s built at Darlington in 1924-25 which at first were fitted with NER style cabs in place of the austere GNR affair. Note the class 2.6.0 painted on the buffer beam, it took Darlington some years to accept the standard LNER class numbers. [F. R. Hebron

UPPER RIGHT: One of the original ten GNR K3s No 4002 stands in Grantham station with a Doncaster-Peterborough local in the early 1930s. [T. G. Hepburn

LOWER RIGHT: Class K3 2-6-0 No 1870 (postwar number) crosses the River Trent as it leaves Nottingham with a Manchester-Leicester train on August 13, 1947. A total of 193 K3s had been built by the time the last appeared in 1937. [T. G. Hepburn

ABOVE: Class K3 2-6-0 No 153 approaches Greenwood box with the 3.35 pm Kings Cross Goods-Niddrie, the famous "Scotch Goods", on September 14, 1934.

[E. R. Wethersett]

BELOW: One of the two handsome Gresley class P1 three-cylinder 2-8-2s No 2394 leaves Potters Bar Tunnel with a New England-Hornsey coal train in 1936. This was the first new design to appear after the grouping and was fitted with a booster on the trailing axle.

[F. R. Hebron]

UPPER LEFT: After the completion of the class J38 0-6-0s with 4ft 8in driving wheels for service in Scotland, Darlington turned to producing a 5ft 2in version which first appeared late in 1926 for general service over most of the system.   Class J39 0-6-0 No 2726 leaves Audley End Tunnel with an up coal train on May 17, 1930.   [E. R. Wethersett

LOWER LEFT: Class J39 0-6-0 No 1974 nears Peascliffe Tunnel as it hurries an engineers special down the GN main line on July 15, 1946.   The last J39 was built in 1941 bringing the total to 289 making it the largest class of Gresley engine.   [E. R. Wethersett

BELOW: In 1927 Darlington produced the first of the three-cylinder class D49 4-4-0s which utilised the same boiler as the J39.   All the D49s were stationed in the northern half of the system with the exception of one based at Kings Cross for a short time.   One of the later engines class D49/2 No 288 *The Percy*, fitted with Lentz rotary-cam poppet valve gear, is seen on arrival at Nottingham Victoria with a Sunday Newcastle-Leicester excursion in 1939.   [T. G. Hepburn

ABOVE: The final lesson learnt from the 1925 GWR-LNER locomotive exchange was the need to increase boiler pressures and in July 1927 class A1 Pacific No 4480 *Enterprise* was fitted with a new 220lb pressure boiler in place of its standard 180lb boiler. No 4480 *Enterprise*, now classed A3, passes Hadley Wood station with the 1.30 pm Kings Cross-Leeds and Bradford express in the early 1930s. Eventually all the A1s were rebuilt with 220lb boilers with the exception of the pioneer No 4470 *Great Northern* which was to receive a far more drastic rebuilding at the hands of Edward Thompson (see page 111). [*F. R. Hebron*

UPPER RIGHT: From 1928 a further series of Pacifics appeared from Doncaster to the improved class A3 "Super Pacific" design. No 2750 *Papyrus* takes water from Langley troughs south of Stevenage with an express from Leeds and Harrogate about 1930. [*F. R. Hebron*

LOWER RIGHT: A gleaming new class A3 4-6-2 No 2746 *Fairway* makes light of the climb from Potters Bar Tunnel with the heavy 5.45 pm Kings Cross-Leeds and Bradford express in 1929. These new A3s were built with left-hand drive after North British drivers had protested about the right hand drive of the earlier A1s. Left-hand drive became standard for all new construction from this date but the older Pacifics retained their right-hand drive until early BR days. [*F. R. Hebron*

ABOVE: Class A3 4-6-2 No 2751 *Humorist* hurries a Kings Cross-Leeds express through Grantham in 1932. *Humorist* was at this time the subject of smoke deflection trials and is seen fitted with a single stove pipe chimney and cutaway smokebox top. *[T. G. Hepburn*

RIGHT: At Grantham the driver of class A3 4-6-2 No 2744 *Grand Parade* awaits the "right away" for York with an express from Kings Cross in the mid 1930s. *[T. G. Hepburn*

BELOW: *Humorist* leaves Barkston with a Doncaster-Peterborough slow train whilst being run in after having been fitted with a Kylchap double blastpipe and chimney in 1937. Because of the soft exhaust small deflector plates as previously fitted had to be refitted the following year. Note the early Gresley GNR articulated set in this train. *[T. G. Hepburn*

Class A3 4-6-2 No 2795 *Call Boy* makes a fine sight as it recovers from a signal check outside Retford with the up "Flying Scotsman" in the early 1930s. The happy choice of race horse names was continued for all the A3 Pacifics. [*F. R. Hebron*

UPPER LEFT: A. J. Hill's GER class N7 0-6-2T was adopted as a standard class and was multiplied from 22 engines to 134. Class N7/2 No 2654 climbs to Potters Bar with the 5.5 pm Kings Cross-Hatfield train about 1930. The train is formed of two Gresley four-car articulated sets and it is said that these "Quadarts" could easily have been converted into electric multiple units should the need have arisen! [F R. Hebron

LOWER LEFT: Class N7/3 0-6-2T No 2603, one of 32 built at Doncaster with round-top fireboxes, awaits its next duty from the east side at Liverpool Street in 1936. This engine is unusual in not having the characteristic GER smokebox door. [C. R. L. Coles

ABOVE: When the need for a more powerful express engine arose for the restricted Great Eastern section, Gresley turned to the North British Locomotive Company who in collaboration with Darlington produced the compact class B17 three-cylinder 4-6-0. Ten engines were built by NBL, the first named *Sandringham* by royal consent, appeared in 1928. No 2803 *Framlingham* climbs towards Brentwood with the 10 am Flushing boat train for Harwich about 1930. [F. R. Hebron

UPPER RIGHT: Class B17 4-6-0 No 2804 *Elveden* overtakes class J39 0-6-0 No 2726 on a Southend slow at Crowlands whilst working a Liverpool Street-Clacton express about 1930. [*F. R. Hebron*

LOWER RIGHT: An unusual duty for a B17, No 2816 *Fallodon* at Marple with the Saturday 2.30 pm local from Manchester London Road on May 2, 1936. No 2816 was allocated to the GC section at this time and could often be seen working the Liverpool-Harwich train through from Manchester to Ipswich. [*R. D. Pollard*

BELOW: Class B17 4-6-0 No 2818 *Wynyard Park* accelerates away from Audley End with the 2.37 pm Liverpool Street-Yarmouth express on August 20, 1935. Only the first sixteen B17s were fitted with Westinghouse pumps out of the 73 built. [*E. R. Wethersett*

ABOVE: Class B17 4-6-0 No 2817 *Ford Castle* passes Trumpington as it leaves Cambridge with the 4.45 pm to Liverpool Street on July 31, 1934. [*E. R. Wethersett*]

BELOW: Class B17/4 4-6-0 No 2866 *Nottingham Forest* about to leave Nottingham Victoria with the 2.20 pm Manchester-Marylebone on June 2, 1939. [*T. G. Hepburn*]

UPPER LEFT: In 1937 two B17s, Nos 2859 and 2870, were fitted with a streamlined casing similar to the A4 Pacifics for working the "East Anglian" express between Norwich and Liverpool Street.   Class B17/5 4-6-0 No 2870 *City of London* is seen at Grantham whilst running in from Doncaster in September 1937.   [*T. G. Hepburn*

LOWER LEFT: Class B17/4 4-6-0 No 2854 *Sunderland*, in wartime black livery, passes Whittlesford with the heavy 5.49 pm Liverpool Street-Cambridge train on August 17, 1943. The final 35 B17s were fitted with standard 4,200 gallon tenders in place of the short 3,700 gallon GE type fitted to the earlier engines.   [*E. R. Wethersett*

BELOW: Gresley class V3 three-cylinder 2-6-2T No 451 leaves Cambridge with the 3.40 pm slow for Liverpool Street on August 11, 1945.   Only a handful of these 2-6-2Ts worked on the GE section for a few years before being drafted north.   The V3 was originally rebuilt from class V1 the only difference being a 20lb increase in boiler pressure from 180lb.
                    [*E. R. Wethersett*

Sentinel 100hp six-cylinder steam railcar No 43301 *Commerce*, towing a six-wheel GNR coach, approaches Bagthorpe Junction on a Pinxton-Nottingham Victoria working on June 2, 1932.   [*T. G. Hepburn*

Another Sentinel six-cylinder steam railcar No 51914 *Royal Forester* waits to leave Hitchin for Hertford North on August 7, 1937.   The 49 cars of this type were all named after famous stage coaches.   [*J. G. Dewing*

Gresley's unique class W1 four-cylinder compound 4-6-4 No 10000, in battleship grey livery, pauses at Grantham with the up "Flying Scotsman" in 1930. No 10000 built in 1929 was fitted with a Yarrow 450lb/sq in water tube boiler.

[*T, G. Hepburn*

No 10000's experimental water tube boiler was not a success and after some years of disuse it was rebuilt in 1937 as a conventional three-cylinder engine with a 250lb boiler, Kylchap double blastpipe and chimney and was streamlined. No 10000 passes Woolmer Green with the 4 pm Kings Cross-Leeds express on June 11, 1938.

[*E. R. Wethersett*

Gresley's celebrated class P2 three-cylinder 2-8-2 No 2001 *Cock o' the North* arrives at Kings Cross with the 10.15 am express from Leeds on May 11, 1935. Built at Doncaster in 1934 for service on the Aberdeen-Edinburgh line No 2001 was fitted with Lentz rotary-cam poppet valve gear, ACFI feed water heater and a Kylchap double blastpipe and chimney. *[K. A. C. R. Nunn. courtesy LCGB*

The second P2 Mikado completed in 1934, No 2002 *Earl Marischal*, leaves Hadley Wood North Tunnel with the 4 pm King Cross-Leeds express in May 1935. No 2002 was fitted with Gresley's conjugated valve gear and dispensed with the ACFI apparatus but owing to its softer exhaust had to be fitted with smoke deflectors soon after entering service. Four further P2s were built in 1936 basically similar to *Earl Marischal* but with the A4 style wedge shaped nose. *[F. R. Hebron*

In 1935 the first of Gresley's famous streamlined class A4 Pacifics appeared from Doncaster painted silver grey in readiness for the inauguration of the "Silver Jubilee" express. No 2509 *Silver Link* is seen in the weighing house at Doncaster in 1936 after modifications had been made to the front-end streamlined casing (see next page). [*LNER*

On Friday September 27, 1935, class A4 4-6-2 No 2509 *Silver Link* passes Potters Bar summit at 75 mph on its amazing debut with the inaugural press run of the "Silver Jubilee". *Silver Link* went on to average 100 mph for no less than 43 miles on end. In August 1936 sister engine No 2512 *Silver Fox* attained 113 mph whilst working the up "Silver Jubilee" and thus attained the highest speed ever recorded on a steam hauled train carrying ordinary fare paying passengers in Great Britain.
[*E. R. Wethersett*

Only four A4 Pacifics were built initially for working the "Silver Jubilee" and although No 2511 *Silver King* was stationed at Gateshead to cover possible failures it sometimes happened that it was not available. On one of those rare occasions class A3 "Super Pacific" No 2501 *Colombo* passes Peterborough North with the 10 am up train from Newcastle on September 27, 1937. *Colombo* was one of the final batch of A3 Pacifics which were built with the "Banjo" dome. [*T. G. Hepburn*

BELOW: Class A4 4-6-2 No 4490 *Empire of India* about to plunge into the smoky depth of Potters Bar Tunnel at Ganwick with the 4 pm down "Coronation" in August 1937. The "Coronation", introduced on July 5, 1937, covered the journey from Kings Cross to Edinburgh in six hours at an average speed of 65.5 mph with the London to York section being reeled off at an average of 71.9 mph. [*E. R. Wethersett*

UPPER RIGHT: Class A4 4-6-2 No 4489 *Dominion of Canada* races past the site of Ganwick box, now replaced by colour light signals, with the down "Coronation" in 1937.   [*F. R. Hebron*

LOWER RIGHT: The beaver tail observation car of the down "Coronation" disappears behind Greenwood box in 1937, the train being hauled by No 4490 *Empire of India*.   [*F. R. Hebron*

ABOVE: Prior to the introduction of the "Coronation" six A4 Pacifics were built at Doncaster for ordinary express duties. These engines were at first turned out in green livery and one of these No 4487 *Sea Eagle*, later renamed *Walter K. Whigham*, stands at Grantham with the up "Flying Scotsman" on May 31, 1937.
[*T. G. Hepburn*]

BELOW: All the A4s were eventually painted in the garter blue livery of the "Coronation" engines. No 4499, formerly *Pochard* and about to be unveiled as *Sir Murrough Wilson*, storms past Belle Isle with the 4.45 pm down "Yorkshire Pullman" on April 22, 1939, passing the pioneer large-boilered Ivatt Atlantic No 3251.
[*E. R. Wethersett*]

ABOVE: Class A4 4-6-2 No 4462 *Great Snipe*, later renamed *William Whitelaw*, crosses Welwyn Viaduct with the 5.45 pm Kings Cross–Newcastle express on July 8, 1939.
[*E. R. Wethersett*

BELOW: Former green-liveried A4 Pacific No 4482 *Golden Eagle* heads the southbound "Flying Scotsman" between Welwyn North and South Tunnels on June 8, 1939.
[*E. R. Wethersett*

UPPER LEFT: The 100th Gresley Pacific which was named after its designer in November 1937, No 4498 *Sir Nigel Gresley* leaves Potters Bar Tunnel with the 4.15 pm Kings Cross-Grantham semi-fast on May 13, 1939.   [*J. G. Dewing*

LOWER LEFT: Class A4 4-6-2 No 4468 *Mallard* one of four A4s built with Kylchap double blastpipe and chimney, departs from Kings Cross with the 5.50 p.m. Leeds express on June 17, 1938.   Driver Duddington, who was to set up the world speed record for steam traction of 126 mph with *Mallard* just over a fortnight later on July 3 is at the regulator.   [*E. R. Wethersett*

BELOW: With its valances cut away the first A4 to be restored to garter blue livery after the war No 4496 *Dwight D. Eisenhower* approaches Potters Bar with an express from Leeds in 1946.   No 4496 was previously named *Golden Shuttle* for working the "West Riding Limited" which linked London with Leeds in 2 hours 44 minutes at an average speed of 67.9 mph.   The outbreak of war in 1939 brought all the streamlined services to an immediate halt, never to be resumed.   [*F. R. Hebron*

UPPER LEFT: The prototype Gresley three-cylinder class V2 2-6-2 No 4771 *Green Arrow* departs from Kings Cross Goods with the 3.40 pm "Scotch Goods" in October 1936.

[*C. C. B. Herbert*

LOWER LEFT: Class V2 2-6-2 No 4774 passes Marshmoor with an excursion from Kings Lynn to Kings Cross formed of M&GN stock (with the exception of one GCR coach) which comprises of former LNWR, MR and GER coaches on June 9, 1937.   [*E. R. Wethersett*

ABOVE: A brand new Darlington-built V2 No 4838 heads south from Newark with an up goods in 1939. V2 Prairies continued to be built during the war years until the class reached a total of 184 in 1944.   [*T. G. Hepburn*

ABOVE: Class V2 2-6-2 No 4817 emerges from Hadley Wood South Tunnel with the down "Yorkshire Pullman" in 1939. This engine was credited with a maximum speed of 93 mph down Stoke bank whilst working the up "Yorkshire Pullman" on one occasion. [C. R. L. Coles

BELOW: Class V2 2-6-2 No 4831 Durham School departs from Nottingham Victoria with a Cleethorpes-Leicester train on August 26, 1939 eight days before war was declared. On the right an unidentified gentleman puts in some practice guard duty. [T. G. Hepburn

ABOVE: Parker GCR class D7 4-4-0 No 5687 passes Littlefield Lane level crossing as it leaves Grimsby with a local train for New Holland on a Winter day about 1930.

[*F. R. Hebron*

UPPER RIGHT: Robinson GCR class D9 4-4-0 No 6014 waits at Retford with a Sheffield Victoria-Cleethorpes train on July 3, 1937. [*T. G. Hepburn*

LOWER RIGHT: Veteran Sacré GCR class D12 4-4-0 No 6466 pauses at Bulwell Common with the Annesley "Dido" in July 1926. [*T. G. Hepburn*

ABOVE: Robinson GCR "Director" class D10 4-4-0 No 5434 *The Earl of Kerry* enters Nottingham Victoria with the 2.15 pm Manchester-Marylebone express in 1932.

[*T. G. Hepburn*]

BELOW: Robinson GCR "Improved Director" class D11 4-4-0 No 5504 *Jutland* passes Harrow on the Hill with a down train of milk empties in 1938.

[*C. R. L. Coles*]

ABOVE: A pair of Robinson GCR class C4 4-4-2s Nos 5262 and 5361 pass Willesden Green with an up excursion bound for Marylebone on August 29, 1933. Both these engines are spoilt by the "flower pot" chimney which Gorton fitted to many GCR engines after the grouping. [E. R. Wethersett

BELOW: One can almost hear Robinson GCR class B3 four-cylinder 4-6-0 No 6169 Lord Faringdon as it slogs past Belle Isle with the 11.10 am Kings Cross-Harrogate Pullman, forerunner of the "Queen of Scots" on July 13, 1926. In the background Ivatt GNR class D2 4-4-0 No 4333 waits with a short goods train whilst two Stirling saddle-tanks pause in their shunting. The B3s were used for a number of years on the GN main line until the Pacifics were allowed through to Leeds. [F. R. Hebron

Robinson GCR class C5 three-cylinder compound 4-4-2 No 5364 *Lady Faringdon* and class D9 4-4-0 No 5110 *King George V* pass Bagthorpe Junction with a Newcastle-Cardiff express on June 2, 1932.　　[*T. G. Hepburn*

Robinson GCR class C4 4-4-2 No 2907 (postwar number) leaves Sherwood Rise Tunnel with a Nottingham-Sheffield local on June 26, 1947.　　[*T. G. Hepburn*

J. G. Robinson produced no less than nine classes of 4-6-0 for the Great Central. One of the first class to appear, B5 No 5180, climbs past New Basford with a Sunday theatrical special from Woodford and the GWR in the early 1930s. [*T. G. Hepburn*

Robinson GCR "Glenalmond" class B8 4-6-0 No 5446 *Earl Roberts of Kandahar* at Nottingham Victoria with a Leeds-Leicester excursion formed of green and cream liveried tourist stock in the mid 1930s. [*T. G. Hepburn*

Robinson GCR "Sir Sam Fay" class B2 4-6-0 No 5426 *City of Chester* takes the sharp curve of the Sheffield line as it departs from Retford with a Cleethorpes-Manchester express in the early 1930s. [*F. R. Hebron*

The Great Central War Memorial engine, Robinson class B3 four-cylinder 4-6-0 No 6165 *Valour* stands in Nottingham Victoria with the 2.15 pm Manchester-Marylebone express in the mid 1920s. [*T. G. Hepburn*

Robinson class B3/2 4-6-0 No 6166 *Earl Haig*, rebuilt with Caprotti valve gear in 1929, heads a down excursion near Northwood in 1938.   Three further engines of this class were fitted with Caprotti valve gear in an attempt to cut their appetite for coal.   [*C. R. L. Coles*

In 1945 Edward Thompson rebuilt No 6166 with two cylinders and a B1 type boiler.   Now classed B3/3 it is seen at Neasden depot, July 7, 1946.   [*E. R. Wethersett*

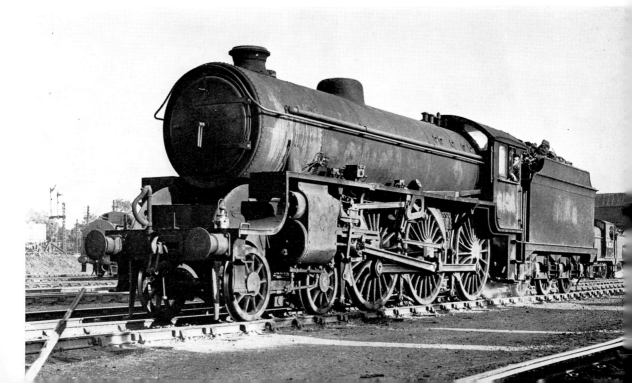

UPPER LEFT: Robinson GCR class B7 four-cylinder mixed traffic 4-6-0 No 5034 slogs up the 1 in 100 east of Dinting on the climb to Woodhead with the 3 pm Ashburys-Grimsby express goods on May 31, 1938.
[R. D. Pollard

ABOVE: Another Robinson class B7 "black pig" 4-6-0 No 5458 heads a freight up the GW&GC joint line on a Winter afternoon in 1938.
[C. R. L. Coles

LOWER LEFT: Robinson GCR class O4/1 2-8-0 No 5404 approaches Sudbury Hill with an up goods in 1938.
[C. R. L. Coles

ABOVE: A Robinson GCR class Q4 0-8-0 eases a Woodford-Annesley haul of coal empties through Nottingham Victoria in the early 1930s. Edward Thompson rebuilt thirteen of these engines as 0-8-0 shunting tanks from 1942.　　　　[*T. G. Hepburn*

UPPER RIGHT: Robinson class O4/3 2-8-0 No 6320 climbs past Crowden with the 71 wagon 11.10 am Godley-Annesley empties on September 29, 1936. This was one of 273 former ROD 2-8-0s purchased by the LNER bringing the total number of O4s to 421, of which 92 were sold back to the WD during World War II.　　　　[*R. D. Pollard*

LOWER RIGHT: Class O4/5 2-8-0 No 6207, rebuilt with a modified O2 type boiler, heads a southbound freight near Whittlesford on July 25, 1933. This was one of the early reboilerings of Robinson 2-8-0s.　　　　[*E. R. Wethersett*

Robinson GCR class L3 2-6-4T No 9067 (postwar class and number) stands near Harrow on the Hill with a permanent way engineers train in 1948. [C. R. L. Coles

Pollitt GCR class F2 2-4-2T No 5785 heads the 2.20 pm Finsbury Park-Alexandra Palace push-pull train near Crouch End on March 30, 1946. Note the third and fourth rails in position for the planned extension of the Northern Line tube which never took place. [E. R. Wethersett

Robinson GCR class C13 4-4-2T No 7418 (postwar number) nears Chalfont & Latimer with the push-pull train from Chesham on October 10, 1948, formed of onetime Metropolitan electric stock. [*J. G. Dewing*

Robinson GCR class A5 4-6-2T No 5158 approaches Northwick Park with the 3.25 pm Marylebone-Aylesbury train on February 22, 1934. [*E. R. Wethersett*

Parker GCR class J10 0-6-0 No 5801 simmers on Chester Northgate CLC depot during the Winter of 1937.
[*E. E. Smith*

Robinson GCR class J11 0-6-0 No 5228 trundles past Bagthorpe Junction with a Woodford-Annesley train of coal empties on June 2, 1932.
[*T. G. Hepburn*

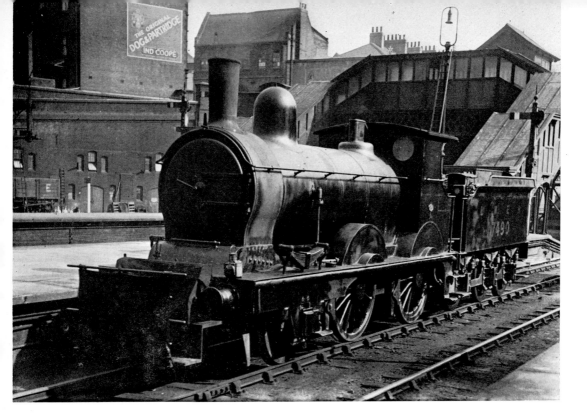

A surprising visitor to Nottingham Victoria was J. Holden GER class E4 2-4-0 No 7490 complete with seat on its buffer beam for judges of the local station gardens competition in 1930.   [*T. G. Hepburn*

J. Holden GER class D13 4-4-0 No 7742 passes Exton Road Sidings as it leaves Kings Lynn with a train for Ely about 1930.   [*F. R. Hebron*

UPPER LEFT: J. Holden GER "Claud Hamilton" class D15 4-4-0 No 1894E (the E suffix was used before the addition of 7000 to the numbers of GER engines) departs from Kings Cross with the 1.45 pm Cambridge train in February 1925. The engine is coupled to a tender originally designed for use behind an oil-burning engine.   [*F. R. Hebron*

LOWER LEFT: During the 1926 miners strike oil-firing was resumed to a limited extent on the GE.   Oil-burning class D15 4-4-0 No 8816 heads the 8.45 am Liverpool Street-Ipswich train east of Romford on July 1, 1926.   [*F. R. Hebron*

ABOVE: Class D15/2 4-4-0 No 8869, rebuilt with an extended smokebox, reaches the summit of the 1 in 70 climb from Liverpool Street at Bethnal Green Junction with a down express in the early 1930s.   [*F. R. Hebron*

Hill GER "Super Claud" class D16/2 4-4-0 No 8783, one of the two Royal engines stationed at Cambridge, heads the 2.4 pm Cambridge-Kings Cross train south of Brookmans Park in November 1938.   [E. E. Smith

Class D16/3 4-4-0 No 8875, in its final rebuilt form with large boiler and round top firebox, waits to leave Ipswich with a Liverpool Street-Felixstowe excursion on July 24, 1938.   [E. E. Smith

S. D. Holden GER class B12 4-6-0 No 8501 approaches Romford with an up train on July 1, 1926. This was one of 25 B12s exiled to the Great North of Scotland section from 1931. *[F. R. Hebron*

Class B12 4-6-0 No 8532 was unexpectedly caught by the camera in 1927 as it toiled up Brentwood bank with a down goods train. *[F. R. Hebron*

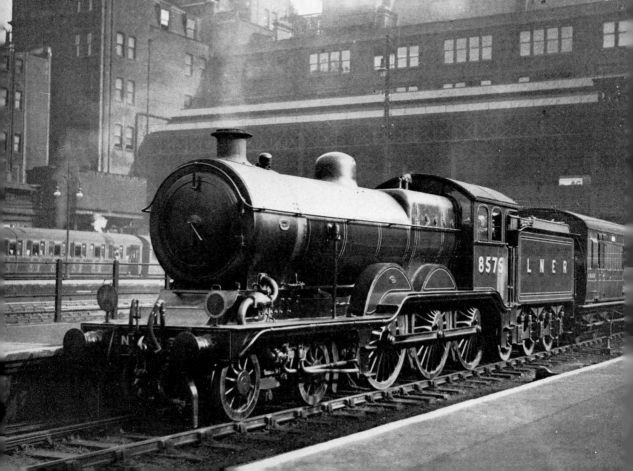

UPPER LEFT: S. D. Holden GER class B12 4-6-0 No 8557 nears Brentwood with a Liverpool Street-Clacton express in the early 1930s.

[*F. R. Hebron*

LOWER LEFT: In 1928 ten further B12s were built by Beyer Peacock with Lentz oscillating-cam valve gear. No 8575 of this series awaits departure from Liverpool Street with a down express on June 10, 1932.

[*K. A. C. R. Nunn, courtesy LCGB*

ABOVE: Class B12/3 4-6-0 No 8530, rebuilt by Gresley with a larger boiler, round top firebox and long travel valves, leaves Hadley Wood North Tunnel with a Cambridge-Kings Cross buffet car express in 1939.

[*C. R. L. Coles*

LEFT: In its final rebuilt form class D16/3 4-4-0 No 8900 *Claud Hamilton* climbs Brentwood bank with the 2.30 pm Liverpool Street - Southend train, Summer 1937. The track had by this date been quadrupled in readiness for the Shenfield electrification which was not completed until after the war.

[*E. E. Smith*

BELOW: Class B12 4-6-0 No 8527, fitted with ACFI feed water heater, approaches Littlebury with the 4.45 pm Cambridge-Liverpool Street on July 27, 1934. Eventually a total of 52 B12s were fitted with ACFI apparatus from 1927 onwards.

[*E. R. Wethersett*

UPPER LEFT: T. W. Worsdell GER class F4 2-4-2T No 7233 arrives at Enfield Town with a "Jazz" train from Liverpool Street formed of two Gresley articulated quintuplets on September 24, 1938. A sister engine waits in the distance to take the train back to Liverpool Street.
[*J. G. Dewing*

LOWER LEFT: S. D. Holden GER class F7 2-4-2T No 8305 waits to leave Palace Gates with the 3.34 pm push-pull train for Seven Sisters, Summer 1938. [*E. E. Smith*

ABOVE: Rebuilt T. W. Worsdell GER class F5 2-4-2T No 7210 (postwar number) leaves Loughton with an Epping train in May 1949 shortly before the extension of the Central Line tube. [*J. G. Dewing*

LEFT: Far from its native country W. Worsdell NER class G5 0-4-4T No 7279 leaves Palace Gates with the Seven Sisters push-pull train in 1948. The use of these engines on the GE was not inappropriate as before joining the NER Worsdell's elder brother was CME at Stratford. [*J. G. Dewing*

BELOW: T. W. Worsdell GER class J15 0-6-0 No 7871 leaves Cambridge with an up pick-up goods on August 19, 1935.
[*E. R. Wethersett*

RIGHT: J. Holden GER class J70 0-6-0 tram engine No 7136 leaves Wisbech with a goods train for Upwell on August 9, 1937. [*J. G. Dewing*

BELOW: J. Holden GER class E4 2-4-0 No 7477 climbs away from Bartlow with the 1.10 pm Cambridge-Haverhill train on September 9, 1943. [*E. R. Wethersett*

BELOW: Hill GER class J20 0-6-0 No 8276 darkens the Cambridgeshire sky as it passes Shelford with an up goods on June 22, 1932. These were the most powerful 0-6-0s on the LNER and were reboilered with round top fireboxes by Thompson from 1943.

[*E. R. Wethersett*

UPPER RIGHT: Ivatt GNR class C12 4-4-2T No 4520 nears Bartlow with the 3.20 pm from Saffron Walden on September 9, 1943. [*E. R. Wethersett*

LOWER RIGHT: Gresley GNR class K2 2-6-0 No 4656 passes through Romford station with an up goods in June 1926. Twenty K2s were transferred to the GE section soon after the grouping whilst another twenty were sent to Scotland. [*F. R. Hebron*

ABOVE: Gresley GNR class K2 2-6-0 No 4679, with outside steam pipes but still retaining a tall GNR chimney, approaches Wood Green with the 5.50 pm Kings Cross-Baldock train in the late 1920s. [*F. R. Hebron*

UPPER RIGHT: Ivatt class C1 4-4-2 No 1459 (GNR number and with early L&NER lettering on its tender) takes water at Nottingham Victoria whilst awaiting departure with the short lived "Sheffield Pullman" for Kings Cross in 1924. [*T G. Hepburn*

LOWER RIGHT: In 1944 Ivatt GNR class D3 4-4-0 No 4075 was fitted with a side window cab and was renumbered 2000 in green livery with crest on its tender for hauling officers' inspection saloons. It is seen here in 1948 near Peascliffe with a Grantham-Lincoln stopping train. [*T. G. Hepburn*

Ivatt GNR class C1 4-4-2 No 3273 passes Wood Green with the 3.15 pm Kings Cross-Leeds excursion in 1925. Note the line of GNR four-wheeled suburban stock whilst above the engine chimney can be seen the twin roofs of Palace Gates GER station.
[*F. R. Hebron*

Rebuilt Stirling GNR class J3 0-6-0 No 4151 pilots an ailing Ivatt class C2 Atlantic out of Grantham with a train of new stock for the "Flying Scotsman" from Doncaster in June 1934.
[*T. G. Hepburn*

Ivatt GNR class C2 small-boilered 4-4-2 No 3950 waits in the centre road at Nottingham Victoria to collect the two through coaches for Leeds Central off a Bournemouth-Newcastle express in 1927.   [T. G. Hepburn

Ivatt GNR class D3 4-4-0 No 4385 pilots class C1 4-4-2 No 4457 on the 1.40 pm Kings Cross-Leeds and Harrogate express seen approaching Cemetery box, New Southgate, in February 1925.   [F. R. Hebron

An immaculate Ivatt GNR
class C1 Atlantic No 4444
attacks the 1 in 107
gradient at Belle Isle as it
makes its exit from Kings
Cross with the 10.45 am
race special for Newmar-
ket on July 13, 1926.
The train is formed of
borrowed Southern Rail-
way Pullman cars still in
the SECR crimson lake
livery.   In later years
Gresley Pacifics worked
these trains right through
to Newmarket, the deepest
penetration they ever
made into Great Eastern
territory.   [*F. R. Hebron*

ABOVE: Ivatt class C1 4-4-2 No 4401 departs from Kings Cross with the 1.40 pm Leeds express in February 1925 whilst an N1 0-6-2T still in GNR livery waits to move empty stock out of the terminus.

[F. R. Hebron

BELOW: A remarkable photograph taken from inside the tunnel mouth at Nottingham Victoria showing class C1 Atlantic No 4420 departing with the Sunday 3.25 pm stopping train for Rugby Central in May 1939.

[T. G. Hepburn

Ivatt GNR class C2 4-4-2 No 3259 accelerates downgrade from Potters Bar with the 1.15 pm Hitchin-Kings Cross local, winter 1937. *[E. E. Smith*

Ivatt GNR class C1 4-4-2 No 4419, fitted in 1923 with a booster on its trailing axle by Gresley, leaves Potters Bar with the 5.10 pm Kings Cross-Hitchin train about 1929. *[F. R. Hebron*

Ivatt GNR class N1 0-6-2T No 4588 departs from Nottingham Victoria with a local train for Mansfield on June 2, 1939. [*T. G. Hepburn*

Gresley GNR class N2 0-6-2T No 4741 leaves Palmers Green with the 8.45 am Kings Cross-Gordon Hill train in July 1928. Despite appearances the N2 had exactly the same boiler as the N1. [*F. R. Hebron*

Ivatt GNR class R1 0-8-2T No 3121 waits for signals at Nottingham Victoria with a coal train from Colwick in 1930. These engines were built for suburban duties in the London area but proved unsuitable. [*T. G. Hepburn*

Rebuilt Stirling GNR class J52 0-6-0ST No 3980 poses beside new A4 Pacific No 4495, not yet named *Golden Fleece*, outside Doncaster Works on September 18, 1937. [*T. G. Hepburn*

Ivatt GNR class Q2 0-8-0 No 3410 tackles the climb from Grantham to Stoke summit at Saltersford with a Colwick-New England coal train in the early 1930s. *[T. G. Hepburn*

Gresley GNR class O1 2-8-0 No 3474 coasts out of Wood Green Tunnel with a New England-Hornsey goods train in 1928. *[F. R. Hebron*

UPPER LEFT: The prototype Gresley three-cylinder engine, GNR class O2 2-8-0 No 3461 climbs from Potters Bar Tunnel with a down goods in the late 1920s. No 3461 was built at Doncaster in 1918 with a rather more complicated version of Gresley's conjugated valve gear than was later adopted for all his three-cylinder engines. Note the inclined cylinders.

[*F. R. Hebron*

LOWER LEFT: A later version of the GNR class O2 three-cylinder 2-8-0, No 3483 passes Three Counties with an up goods on July 8, 1926. A further 41 engines of this class were constructed by the LNER.

[*F. R. Hebron*

ABOVE: Ivatt GNR class J6 0-6-0 No 3628 enters Nottingham Victoria with the empty stock for an evening excursion to Skegness in the late 1930s. The train is formed of London suburban articulated stock, the leading set clearly fresh from overhaul at Doncaster.

[*T. G. Hepburn*

Jones Metropolitan class H 4-4-4T No 107 storms away from Chalfont & Latimer with the 2.20 pm Baker Street-Aylesbury train, Winter 1937. This was one of 18 engines taken over from London Transport when the LNER took over responsibility for working the former Metropolitan steam services north of Rickmansworth in November 1937.

[*E. E. Smith*

Metropolitan class G, now LNER class M2, 0-6-4T No 6156 named after its designer *Charles Jones* at Neasden GC depot on June 25, 1938.

[*J. G. Dewing*

On October 1, 1936, the LNER took over operation of the Midland & Great Northern Joint Railway. The 86 engines taken over were mainly of Midland design and many did not last long under LNER ownership. Rebuilt Johnson M&GN class C 4-4-0 No 55 departs from Sutton Bridge with a Peterborough-South Lynn-Yarmouth train in 1937.

[*T. G. Hepburn*

After the closure of Melton Constable works M&GN locos were overhauled at Stratford where rebuilt Johnson class D 0-6-0 No 069 is seen on February 12, 1938, looking rather uncomfortable in its new livery.

[*E. E. Smith*

UPPER LEFT: The LNER was a firm believer in showing off the company's latest locomotives and rolling stock at exhibitions held in many locations on the system. The scene is at Romford on June 6, 1936, with A4 Pacific No 2512 *Silver Fox* on show together with the Stratford "coffee pot" GER class Y5 0-4-0ST No 7230. In the background spectators are having the unusual experience of being given a "lift" by a steam crane.   [*E R. Wethersett*

ABOVE: Probably the greatest piece of showmanship the LNER put on was the restoration to working order of Patrick Stirling's famous eight-foot single-drivered 4-2-2 No 1 in order to haul a replica of the "Flying Scotsman" of 1888 for comparison with the 1938 version. No 1 is seen departing from Kings Cross on June 30 bound for Stevenage where the privileged passengers changed into the "Flying Scotsman" train of 1938 hauled by A4 Pacific No 4498 *Sir Nigel Gresley*.   [*Fox Photos*

LOWER LEFT: On August 24, 1938, No 1 was used to haul a public excursion to Cambridge and it is seen awaiting departure from Cambridge on its return journey to Kings Cross.   [*J. G. Dewing*

ABOVE: The LNER suffered widespread damage during the blitz of World War II.   Kings
Cross was hit by two 1,000lb bombs which fell on the station offices at 3.21 am on May
11, 1941.   The debris fell on a class N2 0-6-2T standing in the adjacent platform ten with
the stock of a down newspaper train.   [C. C. B. Herbert

UPPER RIGHT: A morning after scene near Ingatestone, where a class B12/3 4-6-0 had
fallen into a bomb crater whilst hauling the 8.45 pm Liverpool Street-Harwich train.   [LNER

LOWER RIGHT: Liverpool Street station was hit several times and on one occasion an
errant LMS wagon was blown onto the roof from Broad Street station.   The view here is
after a bombing raid in 1940.   [LNER

ABOVE: Jones Metropolitan class H2 4-4-4T No 6415 passes a gas spray detector board as it climbs towards Chorley Wood with a Baker Street-Aylesbury train in June 1940. *[J. G. Dewing*

LEFT: Mrs Winzar and Mrs Talbot clean the boiler tubes of Class B17 4-6-0 No 2872 *West Ham United* in October 1942. Women were employed in almost every grade during the war except as shunters or engine crew. *[Fox Photos*

BELOW: The engine that won the war, class V2 2-6-2 No 3655 heads south from Retford on the GN main line with a train load of Churchill tanks in September 1943. *[J. G. Dewing*

ABOVE: The last Gresley locomotive to enter service was the prototype class EM1 1,500V DC Bo-Bo electric built at Doncaster in conjunction with Metropolitan-Vickers in 1941 for the Manchester-Sheffield electrification. In order to test No 6000 it was loaned to the Dutch Railways in 1947 and is seen being shunted onto the train ferry at Harwich by class J67 0-6-0T No 8519.
[Topical Press]

BELOW: No 6000 stands in Naarden-Bussum station, on the Amsterdam-Amersfoort line, at the head of a 405 ton test train in September 1947. The locomotive was nicknamed Tommy by the Dutch railwaymen and the name was officially recognised in 1952 when it had returned to England.
[LNER]

RIGHT: A further 57 class EM1 Bo-Bos were built by BR at Gorton from 1950 in readiness for the completion of the electrification scheme in 1954. No E26037 leaves the new Thurgoland Tunnel, completed in 1948, with a westbound haul of coal on August 9, 1969.
[Brian Stephenson]

UPPER LEFT: In January 1946 work commenced on renumbering the entire fleet of LNER locomotives in a carefully planned scheme of block numbers according to age, type and class. The scheme was originally drawn up in 1943 but it was deemed impractical to carry out in wartime. There were slight alterations to the original scheme, involving the Pacifics and V2s, these were not decided upon until after the renumbering had commenced. Only three engines retained their old numbers, one by design was No 10000 and the other two, Ivatt 0-6-0s Nos 4125 and 4126, by pure chance. Wartime-liveried A4 Pacific No 605 *Sir Ralph Wedgwood*, bearing its new number under the original scheme, leaves Hadley Wood Tunnel with a Kings Cross-Newcastle express in 1946.   [C. R. L. Coles

LOWER LEFT: Class A3 4-6-2 No 98 *Spion Cop*, with its final number after having been No 561 for a short time, passes Greenwood with the 3 pm semi-fast from Kings Cross early in 1947.   [F. R. Hebron

BELOW: The pioneer class V2 2-6-2 No 800 *Green Arrow* recovers from a speed restriction as it enters Wood Green Tunnel with the 1.45 pm Kings Cross-Harrogate train on April 7, 1947.   [E. R. Wethersett

BELOW: In 1946 the LNER purchased a total of 200 war surplus Riddles "Austerity" 2-8-0s from the Ministry of Supply which became class O7. WD 2-8-0 No 77370, later LNER No 3024 and BR 90024, heads an up goods train at Redhall, south of Hatfield in 1947.

[*F. R. Hebron*

UPPER RIGHT: Admirers of Gresley engines were angered in 1945 when Edward Thompson rebuilt the pioneer Gresley Pacific with a 250lb/sq in boiler and three sets of valve gear in place of the conjugated gear. The rebuilt No 4470 *Great Northern* awaits departure from Kings Cross with the 10 am "Flying Scotsman" on July 25, 1946. [*C. C. B. Herbert*

LOWER RIGHT: Another Gresley design rebuilt by Thompson was the B17 4-6-0 of which ten were rebuilt with two cylinders and a B1 type boiler. The first engine to be rebuilt to class B2 was No 1671 *Royal Sovereign,* formerly *Manchester City,* seen leaving Kings Cross with the Royal train conveying King George VI to Wolferton on May 20, 1948.

[*C. C. B. Herbert*

UPPER LEFT: Thompson class B1 4-6-0 No 1096 heads an evening local up the GN main line just south of Welwyn Viaduct in 1947. This was Thompson's most successful design and 410 examples were built between the years 1942 and 1952.   [F R. Hebron

LOWER LEFT: Thompson class A2/1 4-6-2 No 508 *Duke of Rothesay* leaves Welwyn North Tunnel with an evening Kings Cross-Peterborough semi-fast in 1947. The four engines of class A2/1 were originally laid down on the last V2 Prairies but were converted to Pacifics before completion in 1944.   [F R. Hebron

BELOW: Thompson/Peppercorn class K1 2-6-0 No 62036 heads an up goods on the GE Cambridge main line near Littlebury on September 11, 1954. These engines did not appear until 1949 and were developed from Thompson's rebuild of Gresley class K4 2-6-0 No 3445 *MacCailin Mor*.   [E. R. Wethersett

ABOVE: Class A2 4-6-2 No 525 *A. H. Peppercorn* departs from Kings Cross with the 6.5 pm Leeds express on May 13, 1948. No 525 built in 1947 was the first Peppercorn Pacific and was the only member of its class to appear before nationalisation.
[*E. R. Wethersett*

BELOW: Peppercorn's other Pacific design was the new class A1 which did not appear until 1948. The first engine, No 60114 *W. P. Allen*, passes High Dyke as it leaves Stoke Tunnel with a Kings Cross-Leeds express on August 29, 1958.
[*T. G. Hepburn*

LEFT: During the 1948 Locomotive exchanges class A4 4-6-2 No 60034 *Lord Faringdon,* coupled to the NER dynamometer car, departs from Kings Cross with the 1.10 pm Leeds and Bradford express on April 19, 1948.

[*F. R. Hebron*

BELOW: Class A4 4-6-2 No 22 *Mallard* passes through Sonning cutting with the 1.30 pm Paddington - Plymouth express on April 26, 1948. Only the Kylchap A4s were used in the exchanges and they achieved the lowest fuel consumption figures of the trials. [*M. W. Earley*

RIGHT: Thompson class O1 2-8-0 No 63776 in company with the NER dynamometer car, departs from Acton with the 11.20 am freight for South Wales on August 31, 1948. These engines were rebuilt from Robinson GCR class O4 2-8-0s using the B1 type boiler.

[*C. C. B. Herbert*

BELOW: Class B1 4-6-0 No 61251 *Oliver Bury* emerges from Elstree Tunnel with the 10.15 am St. Pancras-Manchester express in June 1948.

[*C. R. L. Coles*

Blue-liveried class A3 4-6-2 No 60052 *Prince Palatine* departs from
Marylebone with the 6.15 pm "Master Cutler" for Sheffield on a summer
evening in 1950.

[*F. R. Hebron*

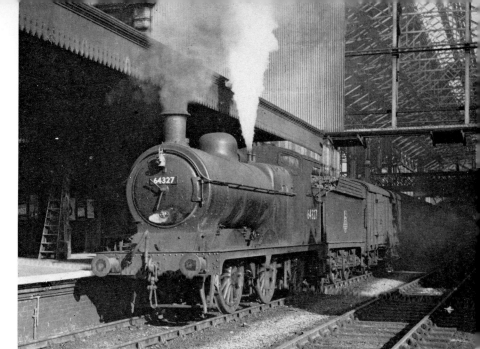

RIGHT: Robinson GCR class J11 0-6-0 No 64327 awaits departure from Nottingham Victoria with a slow train for Leicester on September 17, 1954. Since the closure of the Great Central main line, Nottingham Victoria has been completely closed and razed to the ground.
[J. P. Wilson

BELOW: The last engine of LNER design to work up the GC before its closure in September 1966 was class B1 4-6-0 No 61306, seen leaving Harrow on the Hill with the 8.15 am Nottingham Victoria-Marylebone train on August 23, 1966.
[Patrick Russell

ABOVE: Class D16/3 4-4-0 No 62607 makes a fine sight as it departs from Cambridge with the Kings Lynn portion of the "Fenman" in 1952.
[F. R. Hebron

UPPER RIGHT: J. Holden GER class J17 0-6-0 No 65545 arrives at Rayne with the daily Bishops Stortford-Braintree pick-up goods on March 22, 1958. [J. Spencer Gilks

LOWER RIGHT: Class B12/3 4-6-0 No 61571 heads a Southend-Liverpool Street train near Shenfield on April 24, 1949. [J. G. Dewing

UPPER LEFT: Class B2 4-6-0 No 61632 *Belvoir Castle*, coupled with a tender originally used behind one of the class P1 Mikados, climbs Brentwood bank with a down express on March 24, 1951. [*E. D. Bruton*

LOWER LEFT: Class K3 2-6-0 No 61880 drifts down Brentwood bank with a Clacton-Liverpool Street express in July 1951. The K3 Moguls did not work on the GE until the late 1930s. [*C. R. L. Coles*

ABOVE: Ivatt GNR class C12 4-4-2T No 67379 stands at Stamford Town station with the branch train for Essendine on June 11, 1957. The Essendine branch trains were diverted to the former Midland Town station after the closure of Stamford East GNR station in March 1957, and the entire branch was closed in June 1959. [*J. P. Wilson*

Parker GCR class N5 0-6-2T No 69293 shunts empty stock at Peterborough North on August 18, 1958. These engines replaced the last Ivatt C12s on their duties at Peterborough and on the Stamford-Essendine branch.

[*P. H. Groom*

Ivatt GNR class J6 0-6-0 No 64231 arrives at Twenty with a Bourne-Spalding goods on the last day of the M&GN, February 28, 1959.

[*T. G. Hepburn*

Class V2 2-6-2 No 60817 storms past High Dyke with a Newcastle-Kings Cross express on August 29, 1958.
[*T. G. Hepburn*

In 1957 work started on fitting all the single chimney A4 Pacifics with Kylchap double blastpipes and chimneys on the same lines as *Mallard*.   One of the rebuilt engines No 60013 *Dominion of New Zealand* climbs Stoke bank with the down "Scotch Goods" in June 1962.
[*T. E. Williams*

Doncaster then modified the A3s in the same manner as *Humorist*. A rejuvenated class A3 4-6-2 No 60103 *Flying Scotsman* hurries the afternoon "Talisman" through the newly quadrupled Hadley Wood station on its non-stop run to Newcastle on September 8, 1959.

[*Hunnard Morris*]

BELOW. With the Kylchap A3s the old problem of smoke deflection soon raised its head and after trying the small plates as fitted to *Humorist* in 1932 it was decided to fit all the engines with the "German" style deflectors as seen in this view of 60047 *Donovan* climbing Holloway bank with a down express in August, 1962.

[*T. E. Williams*]

The diesel age is ushered in as class A4 Pacific No 60025 *Falcon* departs from Kings Cross with the Friday 3.10 pm Newcastle via Sunderland express on September 7, 1962. Nine months later on June 16, 1963, the last steam-hauled normal service train departed from Kings Cross hauled by A4 Pacific No 60008 *Dwight D. Eisenhower*.
[*Brian Stephenson*